What Vanishes

JOHN MENAGHAN

salmonpoetry

Published in 2009 by
Salmon Poetry
Cliffs of Moher, County Clare, Ireland
Website: www.salmonpoetry.com
Email: info@salmonpoetry.com

Copyright © John Menaghan 2009

ISBN 978-1-907056-14-7

All rights reserved. No part of this publication may be reproduced or transmitted in any form or by any means, electronic or mechanical, including photography, recording, or any information storage or retrieval system, without permission in writing from the publisher. The book is sold subject to the condition that it shall not, by way of trade or otherwise, be lent, resold or otherwise circulated without the publisher's prior consent in any form of binding or cover other than that in which it is published and without a similar condition, including this condition, being imposed on the subsequent purchaser.

Cover photography: Jessie Lendennie
Cover design & typesetting: Siobhán Hutson
Printed in England by imprint*digital*.net

Man is in love and loves what vanishes

– W. B. Yeats

Acknowledgments

Acknowledgments are due to the following publications in which some of these poems were previously published:

The Adirondack Review, Atlanta Review, Berkeley Poetry Review, nth position, Syracuse Review, & *Working Papers in Irish Studies.*

"Busaras Encounters" first appeared in *Salmon: A Journey in Poetry, 1981-2007.*

I also wish to thank Loyola Marymount University for a 2006 Summer Research Grant that allowed me to complete the book in a timely fashion.

Contents

Out of Place

Going To Jericho	13
An Ordinary Afternoon in Ballybunion	15
In The Buda Hills	19
Coachload, Pass By	20
A Kind Of Blessedness	21
Dingle Suite	23
View From Point Pleasant, 1969	26
Busaras Encounters	27
Dreamtime	31
End There	32

Ardor, and After

Holding Pattern	35
Whatever	37
In Light Of This Morning	38
In Time of the Rattling of Silos	39
Should You Wake	40
Love	41
Flight Distance	42
Warning	43
A Primal Spirit Burning Blossoming	45
Much Love	51
What Did I Care?	52
Buffalo Chips	53
These Days	55
What Vanishes	56

What I Might Be Sayin'

Big Black Cadillac Blues	59
Patti Smith	60
Kissimmee Kid	61
Pyramids	62
Music	64
Monk Alone	66

Objets Trouvés

Genesis	71
The Language Of The Body	72
Opportunity Rocks	73
Words To Live By	75
Sejuiced	78
Chat Line	79
Lost And Found	80
My Life	81

IN MEMORIAM
Raymond Vincent Murphy
1954-1980

Out of Place

*If you get far enough away,
you'll be on your way back home*

— Tom Waits

Going to Jericho

A heron perched on
one leg in the shallows,
scorning a spent force,
what once were waves.

A yellow dog digging
delightedly a deep hole
at the edge of the shore.

The sun warm, not hot;
a breeze curling slowly
over calm English Bay.

Off in the high distance
snow still gleaming
on granite peaks.

Below them white houses
dotted like snowflakes
down the green hills.

Kayakers, windsurfers,
sailboats and big ships
with black and orange
hulls floating flowing
below screaming gulls.

Downtown Vancouver
off to the right, to the left
the Georgia Strait, and
straight ahead Stanley
Park's lush green grove.

I sit on a log on the beach,
behind me The Galley,
its vaguely bluesy music

seeping across the sand,
clashing ever so gently
with the whish of water.

Down to my left two
happy children building
sandcastles with their
father; no mother in sight.

Off to my right a too
tan young man runs
to a motor boat, pushes
it off the sand into still
water, starts the motor,
points the prow toward
someone in trouble one
way or another, I think.

I wait for the sun to sink
behind cold mountains,
drop like a burning stone
sizzling on the surface
of a chilly sea, and hear
Van the Man singing
"Real Real Gone" like
he knows exactly what
he's on about. So do I.

So do I. Middle June.
Vancouver. On this not
quite summer evening.
Sitting on a salty log
on a beach by a pier
in this foreign land
that feels like home.
Hours to go till the day
disappears. Gone to
Jericho. Real real gone.

An Ordinary Afternoon in Ballybunion

County Kerry, Ireland
May, 2006

*Plain men in plain towns
Are not precise about the appeasement they need.*
— Wallace Stevens

I arrive in Ballybunion with time to kill,
never having been in this town before.
Here to give a reading at the local library.
A little hungry, a load of dirty laundry in
the "boot" of my low on petrol rental car.
I find the laundrette, drop off my clothes,
head out to sit on a sunny cliff where
waves curl calmly shoreward in the sun.

Out at Ballybunion Castle I read the plaque
that tells me the Geraldines built this edifice
back in the 1300s, tells me too since then
it's changed hands more than once. I grab
a bench. Sit and watch as workers, golfers,
tourists, businessmen dressed in three-piece
suits drift by or linger, glance at me, move on.

Until an old man, red-faced, white-haired,
spittle glistening on chapped lips, a dirty
tan trench coat a size or three too large
wrapped tight around him, heads my way.
He stops near the bench, gives me the eye,
then sits down at the other end and asks:
So, where are you from yourself?
So much for blending in with the locals,
I think, but say aloud: Los Angeles. L. A.

Hollywood? he says, sounding half pleased
and half scandalized at the same time.
What's it like there? What's all them
movie stars like! I glance at him and smile.
I don't see much of them, I say. At which,
looking disappointed, he turns away.
They're all hiding in their fancy houses,
I add, as if I somehow needed to explain.
Up in the room with a woman, he declares,
facing the sea, anger shaking his frame.
Something like that, I say, not wanting to
exacerbate his condition, whatever it is.

He pivots toward me. What time is it now?
A quarter to one, I say, trying to hide my
pricey watch from view beneath my sleeve.
The news on RTE, he informs me then.
Do you like the Irish news? Wondering
which answer's best I say, doubtfully: I do?
It's good, isn't it, he says, to my deep relief.
But a moment later he's half ordering, half
coaxing me: Go now into one of the pubs
and tell them you need to watch the news!
I will, thanks, I reply, agreeable to a fault.

Standing up, he starts away, turns back.
Goodbye now, he says, as if scolding himself
or me for failing to observe the formalities.
Before I can answer, he asks: How long
are you here? In town, I ask, or in Ireland
do you mean? Here, he repeats, as if to
some simpleton. Here in this town? I say.
Uh, just today. He moves in closer now.
Stares hard. Where else have you been?
In Ireland? I ask. Well, Dublin, Donegal,
Galway, Limerick, Dingle. Moving fast.

He sits again, too close, then moves in
closer, seizes my forearm confidentially.
A beautiful place, Ballybunion, he says.
Natural beauty. The men in suits pass
by again, this time clutching clipboards,
decision makers on a weighty mission.
Men building their buildings, he rasps.
Them building men only muck it up,
the natural . . . setting. The suits afford
him—and me?—a quick, judgmental
glance as they head toward the castle.

When I was a boy some boys I knew
was throwing things at the workers,
he says, his grip tightening on my arm.
Almost caught we was, my friends
and me. Moving still closer now,
gripping tighter still. Men and golf,
he hisses, looking after the suits.
Men up in their rooms with a girl!

Have you ever been up in your room
with a girl, he asks accusingly. Yet
when I turn to answer there's a leer
on his weathered lips, lust lighting up
his bloodshot eyes. Some tourists pass
by the bench, looking faintly alarmed.
What's the right answer? I wonder.
I have indeed been in rooms with girls,
but not here—in Ballybunion, I mean.

Releasing my arm he rises, lingers,
lurches a bit as he goes, looks back.
It's a fine day, he says, a fine day.
It is, I confirm, and watch as he wanders
slowly down the road. When I think
he's gone far enough away, I rise

in turn, take a last look at the ruined
castle and then at the water below,
thinking how many storms must
have battered this beach, how many
old men have moved at this edge
of the world down so many centuries,
how many ruins litter this lovely coast.

Heading for the reading, the library,
I glance back at the bench, knowing
it too must have changed hands many
times over the years, knowing as well
I'll be gone from Ballybunion, most
likely forever—clothes clean, petrol tank
and belly full—when the dazzling sun
slips behind a crumbling castle wall
and disappears into the swirling sea.

In the Buda Hills

At the third floor window of my panzió
the bottom quarter of a tangerine
hangs over Pest, all the rest concealed
behind grey cloud, city lights shining,
shaping a new terrain as darkness falls.
But here below me, closer in, houses
hold their colors, shapes though edges yield
to a buttery blur as night comes on.
Up above, tangerine drifting higher
now till a cloud's grey band splits it in two,
orange glow pulsing above and below
a thin silk sash. Then the hillside fading.
Porch bulbs one by one popping on as dusk
deepens to dark. Tangerine rising against
a charcoal sky till it finally breaks free
and full over Pest's electric sea while
green hills go black at last, landscape aglow
like a milky way full of miniature moons.

Coachload, Pass On

How can I, that woman standing there,
my attention fix
on Yeats' grave or headstone
or the churchyard at Drumcliffe?
For there's a bus conductor knows
only the things he ought,
and here's a load of tourists
that have neither read nor thought.
And nothing that they say is true
about your man—past harm.
But O, that she would quit the tour
And take me in her arms.

A Kind of Blessedness

Late September, Berkeley, and the rains
already come. All afternoon the hiss
of tires past my window as I read, deep
in *Go Down Moses*. Until some urge
impels me into rain. I climb through
mist a street that stretches into hills.
Past houses first, stucco and wood,
stone cupolas and carved mahogany.
But I keep climbing, higher than
I've ever been, up streets and winding
stairs formed out of stone where houses
blend into the branches of old redwoods,
eucalypti, oaks and pines. Fog drifts
above the flatlands, clings to hills,
moves like woven water through the air
and settles high.   The way seems closed.
Beyond the last two houses a dirt path
ravels uncertainly through yellow grass.
Yet still I go—though Faulkner's bear,
and rattlesnakes, are on my mind—
and when I find a fence across my path,
all metal and barbed wire, and then see
down at the bottom a rough circle cut,
I stand and shiver, spend my breath in
parcels, make no move.
                        Will I go through?
Fog drifts through chains. Turning back
toward the city all I see is whited sky
punctured by limbs of scattered trees.
The hole invites me, whispers of release
from all below, and though I see beyond
another fence, and know that to go through
is to go in, not to be gone, I crouch

and slither through damp yellow grass
(as I remember Faulkner's Sam who says:
Be scared, you will be, yes, but you must
never be afraid!) and climb the further
path to one more fence glistening dully,
barbed wire tipped in fog.
                          But am I caught,
afraid, or simply tired when I stop dead
and won't go on? I drop through mist
down muddy paths, my footing more
deliberate than firm, my breath soft-held,
the softer falling rain. Until the landscape
lurches into sight: wet, scattered streets
like wildly woven threads, the storm-dark
bay, the city, Golden Gate, and all in view.
Rain drips off branches down my shirt and spine
—cleansing me, chilling too, stealing my breath—
as if such change of sight and weather were
some fearsome sacrament of blessedness.

Dingle Suite

I. Uisce Beatha

"Ice in the
whiskey?"

"No, no.
Sure it's
not that
hot yet."

II. Full-Time Farmer, Part-Time Forecaster

"Your man on
the telly says
there's to be
an inch of rain,
here, between
now and morning.
I can't see it at all."

III. Seisiún

Musicians are like whores:
they tend to forget
you've been there before.

IV. At the Bar of the Ex-Beauty Queen

"You're here again."
Uncertain smile.
"I seem to be, unless
you're fantasizing."
Slow shake of the head.
"Like a bad penny."
"What?"
"You keep coming back."
"I wonder why."
One head turns.
One sinks down.
A single sigh.

V. Still Life

      Cowblots

                                       of

              colour

black

                                  white

         brown

  on

     a

        deep

             green

                    slope

     only
   the bright
  white house
  ten windows
    blazing
    hinting
   at what
   century
  we're in

View From Point Pleasant, 1969

The night the first men walked upon the moon,
we sat together in a rented room, huddled
near a t.v. set along the Jersey shore.

We children clamored; Mother shushed us quiet.
Outside, the ocean retransmitted light.

Waves reached toward, then crashed below
that cold, reflective stone.

Father fiddled, tried to make it stay:
a ghostly image floating on the screen.

The set lacked an antenna, it was old,
and the round moon within the capsule's view
kept halving, or turned oval, wouldn't hold.

Moments before the moment would have passed,
and we'd have stood before a worthless screen,
Father stood us all together, bound us
in a circle clasping hands, then touched
his free hand to the broken stub
of rabbit ears.
                The picture cleared.
We saw, together, two men walk the moon,
and dared not separate and lose the view.

Now we lie scattered, ten years later,
stretched across a continent and time.

But I recall that circle we once made,
as if to bring the future into view,
and how we stood together hopefully
the night the first men walked upon the moon.

Busaras Encounters

I. In the Waiting Room

Alone on a bench
when an old man
sits down beside me
and after a minute
starts to chat.
I glance at him
briefly but look
away as quickly,
thinking it's money
he'll want in the end.
He goes on for a bit,
then senses my
detachment,
guardedness,
lack of response.

He stares intently at
me for a moment till
I turn and meet his gaze
resignedly, and move my
hand toward my pocket
searching for change to
send him on his way.
His eyes grow sad then
and he says imploringly:
"Don't mind me now;
I'm just an old man
with no one to talk to."

My heart rises to my
throat and my eyes
mist ever so faintly

over as I croak:
"You're alright so."
But whether he's read
my mind or said
his piece, he rises
now and says
goodbye and goes,
slipping down the row,
then out the door.

I sit, abashed, and stare
at all the lonely faces
floating through the room,
waiting alone and chastened
till my coach is called.
Then rise in turn and
gather up my things
and take my leave
of no one as I go.

II. In the Travel Centre

I ask for the young woman I've never met
but need to see about a refund, all our exchanges
up to now having been conducted electronically.
She's off to my left, helping an old lady
book her trip. The old gal seems
a little scattered, and I ask myself
how long she'll likely be, what remains
of youth's impatience rising up in me.

The young one's patient, helpful, but not warm.
"All the cheap fares are gone for Monday, love,"
she tells her customer, who looks alarmed,
breathes six shallow breaths, but then decides.
"Tuesday, now. Would that be better?" she asks.

"Tuesday, Tuesday, let's see, yeah,
Tuesday's grand. Tuesday to Tuesday
is it then?" A long pause, then "Yes."
The young one looks up from the screen
just to be sure. "Yes, Yes," the old one says
to reassure them both. Then starts to stuff
a stack of papers back into her bag.

They're badly folded and so hard to stow.
She tries three times and fails. At last
I say: "Can I help you there?" Just then
she manages to shove them in her little sack,
then smiles at me triumphantly. All seems
well until she tries to slip arms through the straps.
"Could you?" she asks with another, shyer
smile, then turns her back to me. "Of course,"
I say and slide the second strap up her thin arm
till the pack rests between her shoulder blades.
"Thank you," she says. I smile in turn.

The young one hands her up her printed ticket,
turns to me. "Hello," I say and tell her who I am.
Her face lights up then and her voice sends forth
the warmth I'd wished the old one could enjoy.
"Give me a minute now, till I find your file."
The old one turns and says: "They know you here,"
a mix of puzzlement and pleasure on her face
that a Yank should get a warmer welcome than herself.
"They do," I say, embarrassed, then explain.
"It's just because I spend a lot of money,
taking my students out to Newgrange, Galway,
and the like." This satisfies her curiosity
and seems to soothe her ruffled feelings too.
"Enjoy your time here," she says as she moves away.
"And you your trip," I say as she drifts to the door.

"Now, then, how are you," says the young woman,
back with her folder, "are you keeping well?"
"I'm grand," I say, who've learned to talk the talk.
And I'm glad for her warmth and friendliness,
and for still being young enough to notice
that she's cute, and wonder if she's spoken for.
But my mind's mostly on that old one's trip,
which from the look of things might be her last,
and on my parents smiling down at me
who taught me kindness was the great virtue,
and like all virtues its own sweet reward.

Dreamtime:
Somewhere in the Skies
between Sydney & Cairns

> *Il faisait tellement noir à midi*
> *qu'on voyait les étoiles*
> — Picasso

He dreams of stars that never lose their light.
Vast plains of grass that echo distant fires.
Each thin blade lit with verdant afterglow.
Celestial ecstasy sent down the skies.
Of mornings when that light has disappeared
(or seemed at least to vanish in bright air)
down lanes where dew ascends, a cirrus mist,
from packed dirt paths that slowly go nowhere,
winding beneath blue skies littered with clouds,
devoid of rain, that scurry past the sun.

When he awakes it might be night or day
or even dusk or dawn for all he knows.
He casts his eyes about, and understands.
He's still alive. It's all he needs confirmed.
For life means all remains yet possible.
Those stars might still keep spilling endless fire
till time and timelessness at last converge,
exposing death as one more foolish lie.

His eyes close slowly as breath fills his frame.
Behind shut lids the darkness tinges red.
He lies between sleep and sweet wakefulness
and smiles as supernovas blow his brains
across the universe inside his head
and light rains down till no dark realm remains.

End There

for Samuel Beckett

no end
no there
no wind
no air

all ends
somewhere
pretend
it's here

Ardor,
And After

Therefore is love said to be a child
Because in choice he is so oft beguiled
– Shakespeare

Holding Pattern

Lying on the couch together,
neither, quite, lovers nor friends.
Lying and telling the truth
at the same time but refusing
to lie, together, about some
matters, what matters most:
the truth of what they feel
lying there in each other's arms,
trying to hold each other
at arm's length, yet hold on
tight, trying to keep each other
from harm. Not *I can't live
without you* but *I don't want to*.
Not *I don't love you* but *How
can I?*—things being what
they are—in a word, bizarre.
To feel so much lying there
between them and yet know
all their loyalties lie elsewhere.
The truth of that laid between
them like a sword, yet embracing
all the same who and what and
where they are, holding to what
they know, what they can do,
and hoping to somehow find
a clear way through. Lying,
together, on the couch in
the long afternoon, the living
room, holding each other's face
between trembling hands, adrift
in the fathomless depths of one
another's eyes, flesh breathing
against warm palms. Struggling
to hold so much inside, yet

effortlessly holding each other's gaze as if their souls were now forever intertwined. Lying and telling the truth till it slashes deeper than any sword. Lying together on a couch, neither quite lovers nor friends, dying to see this through and still somehow never see it end.

Whatever

Look.
Here it is.

We'll sleep together.
We won't sleep together.
We'll be friends.

Things will get better.
Things will get worse.
We'll be friends.

It'll rain.
It'll snow.
There'll be
earthquakes,
tidal waves,
fires, floods,
hurricanes,
cyclones.
We'll be friends.

Whatever happens.
Whatever doesn't.
Whoever does what
to whom or with
whom, whenever,
wherever, however.
We'll be friends.

Got it?
Good.

Now can we
please go
to bed
together
please?

In Light of This Morning

Coffee steams near two
late projects. You type.
I proofread. The frown
you're wearing clashes
with your nightgown.
The harsh, clicking
keys stand in for
your piccolo voice.

Morning is your worst
light, and you know it.
Armed with reluctance,
you are seldom magnificent
before noon. Yet ten-thirty
or so on this Saturday
morning, I see you rise
above your morning self.

When I mention your
tendency to spell
"guise" with a "q,"
your smile blazes
like a five-alarm
fire. Ten ink-
smeared fingers
shoot a laser hex.

I lift a coffee mug
in mute salute, and
fog my glasses.
You grab it, gulp,
and clarify my view.

In Time of the Rattling of Silos

Love, if the world should shatter into bits
And scatter every atom, some being split,
Our dust would drift into another part
Of endless space, souls find out other hearts.

Let us choose now, while chances multiply,
To forge new paths across the shapeless sky,
To flame in orbits through the startled night,
Engrave the dark with signatures of light.

The play is on, the scenery all arranged.
With more time there are lines we'd want to change,
But it will be enough to step and dance
Across the creaking floorboards. There's a chance

Before we slip out of our present shapes
To take these bodies, minds, and watch them trace
Their progress through our playlet while it lasts.
Like sleek heat-seeking missiles, burst and blast

Across this crazy cosmos side by side
As if there were no way that we could die.
Or trickle, sweet slow streams, directionless,
Whittling a path through matter, randomness.

Should You Wake

Should you wake before me
you will find this sheet
on the kitchen table.
The note paper swims under
script like an ocean of snow,
cooler than the notes floating
from a jazz piano, cooler
than this midnight summer air.

You lie in bed one room away.
I'm joining you soon; lie still.
But the plants look wonderfully
grown and green, potted along
the windowsill; and the tumbler
clicks in a firm, decisive manner
as I bolt the door for sleep.

The carpet stretches, yawns
from wall to wall, curtains hang
limp, dependent on their rest,
and the couch is depressed
from lying under me.

Should you wake before me,
you will find these words.

Love

Love is recognition, not desire:
Eyes that cannot look away or down.
The only fire that feeds and feeds on fire.

Lust is what the lost feel, love the found
Who neither would possess nor be possessed.
Love is recognition, not desire.

Lovers glow in air, but tread on ground:
Wet earth their brilliant bodies burn and bless.
The only fire that feeds and feeds on fire.

Love, traveling between them, makes no sound.
Silent each look, sigh, shiver, or caress.
Love is recognition, not desire.

Eyes lost in eyes, light piercing depths profound.
Entrancement of fierce flames disdaining rest.
The only fire that feeds and feeds on fire.

Consuming nights and days in endless round,
They know what others never think to guess:
Love is recognition, not desire.
The only fire that feeds and feeds on fire.

Flight Distance

> *The distance an animal needs to retreat from*
> *an approaching creature in order to feel safe;*
> *the size of the cushion of empty space*
> *it wishes to maintain around itself.*

Snug in my bed, the comforter around you,
you feel safe. Tired of trying, for tonight,
to reconcile your competing needs
for contact, distance, intimacy, space.

Next morning, waking in what's still to you
despite so many nights a stranger's bed,
and finding me asleep against your back,
you'll feel a sudden impulse to retreat.

You'll rise and dress in cool, crisp morning air,
wake me enough to take your leave, and go,
trusty old bicycle between your legs,
pedaling away from danger to your place.

Later, I'll wake to find the note you've left,
yellow paper on the cold white stove,
and shiver as I read your too few words,
feeling so safe and empty I could weep.

Warning

You left behind a loaf of bread,
half-baked in an unreliable oven,
saying I might want to put it back
in a while and see if that helped,
then headed off to spend a weekend
visiting the life that you'd once led.

I burned the bread. Not purposely
but out of mindlessness, distraction,
what you will. Then scattered it,
later, over the lawn where I'd hung
the laundry, yours and mine together:
shirts, socks, stockings, underwear,
trousers, shorts, towels and sheets.

And standing at the window watched
in quick succession three species appear
in reverse pecking order, careful not
to seize the bread too quickly lest some
clever trap might catch them unawares.

The battered sparrows first, scanning
air and ground with nervous thrusts.
Orioles next, surveying from the fence
what might be stolen safely. Then black
crows, dropping like bits of darkness,
chasing away the smaller birds before
condescending to take a share and more.

I stood there wondering had some secret
signal been broadcast when one lone
sparrow sighted food? Did they have
a sound for bread? Or had they been
each on its own patrol? Did the sparrows

or the orioles resent the pushy crows
—all bluster, lustrous black wings
flapping faster than laundry on the line?

The crows took all they wanted, then sped
skyward one by one, or in small groups,
till only one black speck still flecked
the emerald lawn. When suddenly that
last gloating crow ascended and let loose,
smattering crap across our snowy sheets,
flew straight at my window, veered
at the last split second, disappeared.

I looked back over at the oven then,
thinking: some love is like this,
half-baked, soft-cored, underdone.
Or over: burnt, broken, tossed across
a sodden lawn while the faint sun
shines and breezes blow. Scattered
fragments of fine intent, destined in
the end to feed only the ignorant who
live by bread alone, or think they do.

This is a warning, love, just a warning,
only a warning, but a warning still.

A Primal Spirit Burning Blossoming

I.

In a pavilion filled with paper light
I stood alone before a painted screen,
*Pheasants amid Bamboo and a Blossoming
Plum Tree*, listening to water flow,
looking straight ahead, seeing only you.

Then fumbling in my pockets found a dime,
and made a wish, and tossed it in a pool,
above which spread, across gold-leaf background,
thin brown branches where a pheasant perched.
The wish I made was this: that you and I
would be together soon, and then always.

I watched the ripples run from that thin dime,
then stared down where stilled silver dully gleamed,
wanting to know what chance such a hope had,
searching for signs my vain wish might come true.

II.

Returning up the sloping ramps to meet
the friend I'd come with, I seized one more chance,
eluding her, to make another wish,
this time before a hanging paper scroll:
Cliff, Moon, and Autumn Grasses. It was small
compared to the hinged screen where I'd first wished.

My wish was smaller, too. I stood and tossed
another dime, eyes closed, into the pool
and wished, if by chance we were not to be
together soon, and then for all our lives,
that I might find a way to let my love,
so boundless, somehow find its proper form.

I stared hard at those ripples, too, that dime,
wondering if this wish had some better chance.
Then hit the shop, bought a note card for you.
As change, the cashier gave me back two dimes.
Did this mean that my wishes were refused,
or that at least one of them would come true?

III.

My friend was eager to see everything,
so we left to check out *A Primal Spirit*,
some avant-garde exhibit, but my soul
still lingered by those paintings, wanting you,
and wondering how my wishes were to fare,
and how you'd be when in a mere few days
you came back home after too long away.

Yet wandering in this daze of wondering
I found myself before a ring of wood
burnt to a blackness, and inside that ring,
a second perfect circle formed from bronze,
and stood and shivered, tingling head to toe,
took two steps back, and sat, and stared it down.

Then my friend found me, wordlessly sat down
across the room and stared herself upon
another burnt bright mass of stone and bronze
made by the same man, and like those two works
we balanced one another, sitting there.

IV.

The day before we'd sat, this friend and I,
in yet another gallery, before
a Rembrandt portrait of Titus his son.
Unfinished and yet so breathtaking I'd
imagined stealing it, then hanging it
above the bedstead of the child I crave
to make and raise with you. Imagined too
holding you, staring down at our sweet child,
while Titus gazed out at us in his turn.
Unfinished, as our love may always be,
as children are, as I am without you.

Standing beside my friend then, feeling things
I could have shared with no one else but you,
I'd asked her if she thought she wanted kids.
She thought she did but didn't know with whom
and seemed a little sad not to know more.

Then as we left the gallery we'd found
awaiting each of us a parting gift,
a child for each, a print of the Rembrandt,
and looked at one another wonderingly,
and I'd said: "Each of us will have a child,
that must be what it means." And we'd both smiled.

V.

Having stared long and hard at that charred ring,
I made excuses now, went back to look
in the pavilion at the dimes I'd dropped
and at the paintings, which seemed to contain
competing fates for me within their frames.

I went back first to *Pheasants amid Bamboo*.
Slender green stalks set off against the light
brown branches, purplish plums; pheasants half-hid
among the ivory flowers and leafy gold.
I looked down at my dime, and then looked back
at what now struck me as a family,
five pheasants frolicking in golden light,
and thought: a life with you would be like this.

Tearing myself away, I headed toward
Cliff, Moon, and Autumn Grasses to confront
a different destiny: a miniature
in muted colors, beautiful but stark.
Limned solitude. A chilly loveliness
in which the grasses did not grow but pierced
like spear points a flat, frosty disc of light,
and the black cliff, grey moon, green grass all hung
in austere autumn beauty, cold and dark.

Thinking of you these last few days I'd found
a phrase kept running through and through my head.
Love, I would walk through fire to be with you.
But now I'd seen two fates pictured for me
by masters from another century
and half a world away—one cold and dark,
but beautiful, as solitude can be,
and the preferred one: golden, blossoming.
How could I know which fate awaited me?

VI.

Anguished, I stumbled back to Lotus, those
charred circles, stared hard, penetrated to
the heart of their creation, hidden core.
Quintessence their creator sought to grasp
by burning what he'd made to a black crisp.

I moved, not moving, through those perfect rings:
wood and brass wedded, cool concentric flames.
I walked, not walking, through two blazing bands.
Imagining that it might never matter.
Then that it would, and that when I emerged
you'd be there and embrace me and we'd burn
forever and forever and yet be
beyond the reach of fire's ravages,
one body blossoming, two souls aflame,

and stood burning for you, calling your name.

Much Love

Much love she always
with a flourish signed
each card and note
she sent his way.

Leaving him to
wonder, silently,
how much exactly?

The time came when
he knew the answer
all too well, making
him regret he'd always
been afraid to ask her.

What Did I Care?

What did I care what the moon might do,
adrift in a sea of endless stars?
When I look at the moon, I remember you.

Look, look, you'd say, *at that moon and those stars!
Oh, how they glow, but the moon especially.*
What did I care what the moon might do?

*Is it waxing or waning? I can't tell.
Can you? Will it fade or grow? Do you know?*
When I look at the moon, I remember you

wanting nothing more than to gaze and gaze
—at it, not me! Fascination misplaced?
What did I care what the moon might do

when we could be locked in each other's arms,
burning bright as suns in a midday sky?
When I look at the moon, I remember you.

Now you've vanished, like all those nights and days
and the chance to be everything to me.
What did I care what the moon might do?
When I look at the moon, I remember you.

Buffalo Chips

Because there is no love, the children dance.
Regulars at this rodeo of drunks
nodding to their numbers, checking out
two newcomers doing their best to seem
hip to whatever's happening. Not much is.
A waitress slipping through the tangled crowd
proffering shots of something for a buck:
pink vials trembling in a cardboard tray.
A disk jockey, headphones on one shoulder,
looking like your classic high school dork.

The bartenders keep one eye out for tips,
one on the slow clock, and the bouncers thread
menacingly through the flotsam on the floor.
Above the noise a voice: "Bobo, front door.
Come to the front door, now!" And one old man,
red-faced, clutching a lite beer in one hand,
a lit weed in the other, sleeps it off,
oblivious, smiling, propped against a wall.

The dancing's all just sex. There's not a trace
of deeper feeling in one single face.
Women in miniskirts and open shirts
sprouting lingerie along their legs,
looking seductive as all hell and yet
screaming "don't touch" with the same sultry glance.
Men on the prowl, turned out in leather, silk,
or clad in denim, plaid, cowboys at heart,
just looking for another lay, another beer.

The friend who dragged me here wishes he were
back with his ex-wife, child, a continent
away. I wish that I were home in bed,
preferably with a woman I could love.

But we don't say such things. Instead, we say:
"What a scene," "Wild, huh?" "Interesting
crowd," "Oh, yeah," and "So, want another beer?"

I think of those few women that I've loved,
love still, if truth be told (it always will),
but who aren't home, who aren't anywhere
waiting for me. And think, too, of the chance
in which I still believe, my scars aside:
to love one woman the rest of my life,
be loved back the same way, the same amount.

My friend asks if I want to stay or go.
As if it made a difference, I say "Go."
After ten minutes we're still standing there.
Looking at women we don't really want.
Thinking about the long, cold night ahead.
Gulping down our pride. Guzzling our beer.
Like all the rest, we'd be hard pressed to say
what the hell we think we're doing here.

These Days

These days each place he leaves he leaves alone.
Though not by choice, a solitary man.
Or is it choice, a part of some grand plan?
Is he still thinking he might find the one?

No one can say. Not even he who roams,
searching for who knows what, or sits and broods
on what he's done wrong, why this solitude
is all he leaves with, all he brings back home.

What Vanishes

Man is in love and loves what vanishes
— W. B. Yeats

What vanishes everything
all one loves or doesn't
but does love o no love
endures all loss if it be
true loss makes it but
more real more felt more
helpless to desist despite
decease of all it loves
as it all goes the way
of flesh and all things
born or made love is
a blade that cuts thru
loss and grief not holding
on but giving all the same
it's all beyond the fall all
loved things disappearing
without trace love lasts
beyond the loved sight
shape effaced beyond all
knowing love keeps going
yet stays still power without
will but to survive all even
loss of all it loves no
vanishing can vanquish
love nor love itself restore
all that's been lost o no
love has no power but to
endure endure endure
love is in man and woman
and all things and all
things vanish all but love
in love with man and
woman and all things
loving what vanishes
everything all but love

What I Might Be Sayin'

*After silence, that which comes nearest
to expressing the inexpressible is music*
— Aldous Huxley

You know what I might be sayin'
— Lightnin' Hopkins

Big Black Cadillac Blues

for Lightnin' Hopkins

Chasin' the blues and
a black honey too
callin' come on back
with my black Cadillac
bent over battered wood
you pick a motor hum
from quiverin' strings
chalky fingers sing
those Cadillac blues
chasin' that dark fox
stole your wheels
wicked-quick fingers
slow-tappin' heel
club full of honkie
hipsters listenin'
while you holler
teeth glisten like
that Caddie's white
wall tires spinnin'
tales and riffs with
a sorrowful grin
collectin' on old
Lightnin's dues
servin' up your
stew of blues
laughin' like all
you might lack
is that big black
dream Cadillac

Patti Smith

*(Photograph by
Robert Mapplethorpe)*

Rodeo queen, stallion rider,
the image of the heroin.
Against a grey milk background:
frail waif, black disheveled
mane, suspendered androgyne.

Voice that shrieks and wobbles,
stomps and shouts, wavering
like a jug band saw combed
up-tempo to the old rock beat.

Mick Jagger mouth, ragsleeve
shirt, white wrists emerging.
Insolent, tough dark eyes
announce the ominous challenge:
"Do you know how to pony?"

Long, curved fingers clutch
a blazer draped across
one shoulder, galloping
stallion pinned to the lapel.

Things you would not expect
to find: wrong-fingered
wedding band, delicate
wristwatch held with
a shoestring strap.

Pale album cover backdrop,
picture cropped at the hip.

Kissimmee Kid

for Vassar Clements

You fidget under stage light,
choke the slender neck
between thick fingers.
The bow pops onto strings
and slides. That lonesome,
fitful range you pick
resounds in shallow wood
while crowd hands clap
a beat you never touch
but glide above. Banjo
tings and twitters on
high wire. Fiddle wails
like brakes on a pick-up
careening through the hills.
Farm boy hands that never
fret. The screech of every
crop was ever picked, of
every chicken ever plucked.

Pyramids

for Pharaoh Sanders

O
no
I've
heard things
louder than Pharaoh's
horn just can't remember
when softer a second then
booming again hard not to pay
attention what hard bop hard to say
old Pharaoh playin' his own way building
up walls note by note pyramids of pleasure
jewels hidden deep inside a wonder of this world
or any other mother fucker better listen up you hear.

I
saw
him play
at Catalina's
back in the day
sitting at the bar
not him fool me while
he blew up the room boom
boom down in front everybody
duckin' for cover or clutchin' their
lover if they got one or their drink instead
just glad either way they ain't dead o no more alive
than ever no jive that dude plays his sax like a bazooka
blam blam blam blam blam blam blam toot toot boom boom.

Do
you even
know what I'm
talking about I'm sayin'
he's a stone cold killer with
a gleaming horn spraying bullets of
sound all over town hell all over the goddamn
universe at the end of the night they pull up a hearse
to the back door of the club and carry out the dead dudes
who listened so hard they had some kind of stroke it ain't no
joke I'm telling you now don't you dare say you wasn't warned
Pharoah rules the roost simple as that you in his sights splat splat
no escape hell everybody dies not yet don't fret he's got another set.

Music

*for Ernestine Anderson,
and for Karen*

Does music make us over
or make up for all we've
missed, or all endured?
Yes, perhaps, sometimes
yet when Ernestine steps
down from the bandstand
after her last set while
half the crowd makes for
the door, the other half
lingers, muttering praise
vaguely in her direction,
and a few brave, flush souls
who bought her tape at the bar
sidle up for an autograph and
when your turn comes she looks
at you—this woman it would be
hard to say exactly how old,
beautiful maybe but hard, hard
times carved like hieroglyphs
at the corners of sleepy eyes—
looks at you, then the man
you're with, a younger man,
then back at you, and smiles
a knowing, saying smile saying
I know where you been, honey,
it wasn't easy for you and me
to meet here tonight, been
a long, long road, and you
got yourself a young thing,
good for you, and you think,
well, but Ernestine, you got

the music, smiling too, saying
nothing, proffering a pen and
she sighs and signs and says
to one of her handlers Honey,
get me a drink, will you, please
and heads for a table and sinks
down onto the chair, you can see
the music's all gone for tonight
and she's left with the knowing,
the years, and the smile fading
to blankness, and you know, don't
want to know but know the music
is only the music while it lasts,
leaving her when it leaves with
all the rest to face, too tired
to dance, and your heart sinks
down with her there even though
you wouldn't have wanted, not
for the world, to miss a note.

Monk Alone

for Thelonius Monk

Monk alone at the piano
pushing pedals to the floor
kissing keys with a feather
touch skin barely feeling
the fleeting caress of cool
ivory rising up against
his fingertips as they flee
pursuing new chords as if
melody moved forever further
but never quite out of reach
making him stay on the bench
bent over the board never for
a moment bored never lost
because destinations don't
matter now nothing matters
but moving through the maze
no voices now demanding
directing intruding into his
sweet chaotic solitude no rude
producers saying how about
playing it this way or that
getting fat on his dreamy
acute demanding dexterity
nothing to seek or find
or welcome or mind or
ask for or give no whirring
blenders behind the dim lit
bar at the back of some club
or some fool drunk on the
sound of his own voice
talking over the notes no
struggle to rise above

the goddamn ambience
cover charge profit motive
waitress waiting for her
shift to end so she can
spend the night wrapped
in the arms of some man
who fails to appreciate
her finer qualities none
of that in Monk's head
now alone secluded in
sound until it all comes
down to one last flourish
so quiet his ghost fingers
scarcely move as smoky
notes drift along a spotted
ceiling and dissolve a
broken spell a hushing
deep inside his soul.

Objets Trouvés

*We always find something, eh, Didi,
to give us the impression we exist*
— Samuel Beckett

Genesis

(from Diane Arbus)

In the beginning
of photographing
I used to make
very grainy things
I'd be fascinated
by what the grain
did because it would
make a kind of tapestry
of all these little dots
and everything would be
translated into this
medium of dots
skin would be
the same as
water would be
the same as
sky and you
were dealing
mostly in
dark and light
not so much in
flesh and blood.

The Language of the Body

(from a video catalogue)

Humans can make more than 3,000 hand gestures, but even the simplest, according to Desmond Morris, has numerous variations and interpretations. This program catalogs not only hand gestures, both friendly and insulting, but facial expressions, head shakes, and body distance as well—and the misunderstandings that can occur when body language is transported across cultural lines. Suppression of body language is also discussed, along with "nonverbal leakage," in which the body's language can belie a speaker's words. Some gestures may be objectionable. Contains nudity. Not available in French-speaking Canada.

Opportunity Rocks

(in a restaurant window)

we are looking
for a great
bar manager
are you
passionate
about booze
can you manage
a team
be happy
to work hard
do you like
the excitement
of late nights
can you make
cocktails
do you
seek the thrill
of making people
drink
do you
love wine
are you
together
are you
looking
for a long-term
gig
in a good
venue
if you
answer
yes

to these
questions
look
no further
this
is your
job
apply
within

Words To Live By

(from a calendar)

"Honesty is
the first
chapter in
the book
of wisdom"
Thomas
Jefferson
"Give the
American
people a
good cause
and there's
nothing they
can't lick"
John Wayne
"Rather fail
with honor
than succeed
by fraud"
Sophocles
"Once you
learn to love
you will have
learned to live"
Unknown

There's nothing
of honesty
in the book.
Honor is
to live with
wisdom

and people.
Give Thomas
Jefferson the
Unknown American.
Once you learn
the first chapter
in Sophocles
you will have
learned they
can't lick
a good cause
by fraud.
Rather than
succeed, fail
to love
John Wayne.

Sophocles
can't lick you,
Thomas
Jefferson.
Honesty is
nothing.
In the book
there's a
chapter of love
and the first
good cause.
The American
People learn
to fail
by fraud
rather than
succeed with
honor.
Once you
live unknown,

they will
have learned
to give John
Wayne wisdom.

John Jefferson
learned to
love the
American in
the first chapter.
Will you have
Wayne Thomas
fail unknown
rather than
live with
honesty?
Give
people
a book
of Sophocles.
Wisdom is
nothing they
can't lick.
Once
succeed
by fraud
and there's
the good
cause
you learn
to honor.

Sejuiced

(in a shop window)

Have you got
a good sense
of humor?
Are you
enthusiastic?
YES!!!
Then we
are looking
for you.

We need
someone
three days
per week
flexible
hours
fair
pay.

You will be
required
to dress
in a fruit
costume
advertising
our all
fresh juice
bar place
of work
shop
street
if you are
interested?

Chat Line

(in a bus shelter)

I.

"Are you living
with Autism?
Do you want to
talk to someone?
Call Autism
Link now.
You don't have to
go it alone!"

II.

Are you living?
With Autism?
Do you want to?

Talk to someone.
Call Autism.
Link now.

You don't have to!
Go it alone!

Lost and Found

(from a fortune cookie)

"Your lost possession
will be found
within the month."

Your lost month
will be the
possession found within.

The month, found
within your possession,
will be lost.

Your lost will?
The found month?
Be within possession.

My Life

(from Teilhard de Chardin)

and
 so
for
 the
first
 time
in
 my
life
 perhaps
I
took
 the
 lamp
 and
 went
 down
 to
 the
 inmost
 self
but
 as
 I
 moved
 further
 and
 further
from
 the
 conventional
 certainties
 I
became

aware
that
                                I
                            was
            losing
                                                contact
    with
            myself
                        at
                            each
                                        step
of
        the
                descent
                        a
                            new
                                        person
was
        disclosed
                    within
                        me
                                            . . .
and
        when
                I
                    had
                            to
                                    stop
my
        exploration
                        because
                            the
                                        path

faded
 I
  found
   a
   bottomless
   abyss
   at
   my
   feet
    and
     out
      of
       it
came
 arising
  I
   know
    not
whence
 the
   current
    which
  I
   dare
 to
  call
  my
  life

About the Author

John Menaghan, born in New Jersey, has lived in Boston, Berkeley, Vancouver, Syracuse, London, Dublin, Belfast, Galway, Gortahork, and Dingle, & presently makes his home in Venice, CA. Winner of an Academy of American Poets Prize and other awards, he has published poems and articles in various journals and given readings in Ireland, England, France, Hungary, and the U.S. He has also had several short plays produced in Los Angeles. Menaghan teaches at Loyola Marymount University in Los Angeles, where he also serves as Director of both the Irish Studies and Summer in Ireland programs and runs the LMU Irish Cultural Festival.